1978

# The
# Rainbow Grocery

William Dickey

The University of Massachusetts Press   Amherst, 1978

"George," "Chickens in San Francisco," and "Face-Paintings of the Caduveo Indians" first appeared in *New Letters.*
"A Kindness" first appeared in *The New Yorker.*
"The Death of Mr. Thrale" and "The Poet's Farewell to His Teeth" first appeared in *Poetry.*
"Killing to Eat" and "Alligators and Paris and North America" first appeared in *The Massachusetts Review,*
© 1978 The Massachusetts Review, Inc.

Library of Congress Catalog Card Number 78-53381
ISBN 0-87023-252-5 (cloth): 0-87023-253-3 (paper)
Printed in the United States of America
Designed by Mary Mendell

Library of Congress Cataloging in Publication Data
appear on the last page of the book.

For
*Adrianne and Warren*
*and for*
*Jacqueline and Peter*

Acknowledgments

Some of the poems included in this collection have appeared in
*Aisling, The Chicago Tribune Magazine, Foothill Quarterly, Impact, The Iowa Review, The Massachusetts Review, New Letters, The New Salt Creek Reader, The New Yorker, Ploughshares, Poetry, Poetry Now, Poetry * Texas, Quanta* and *Thirst*. Some
of the poems have also appeared in *Sheena*, a booklet published
by the Funge Art Centre, Gorey, County Wexford, Ireland. Completion of this book has been assisted by a sabbatical leave
granted by San Francisco State University, and by a fellowship
in creative writing awarded by the National Endowment for
the Arts.

# Contents

# One
## In the Dreaming

To the Collector of Taxes, City and County
of San Francisco


No, there is no dog, terrier, male, dog's name Pedro
at this address. Pedro is in San Anselmo.

So I do not owe you the $4.00 license fee
(raised by the Supervisors to $5.00). I wish I did.

Is the point of being a poet to clean your plate,
use up things, make every loss valuable?

And when the last loss has been made valuable
disappear like night into the crouching wood?

I like you because you are such a plain image. You seem to say
if I pay my tax there is something I can own

for another year. There's nothing. There's no dog.
But thank you for even suggesting that there is.

## Powers of Five

Keep pushing the
X button on the printing calculator
and it will
give you successive powers:
5, 25, 125.

What do they
translate into?
Five fish
then twenty-five fish,
five to the second power.
I am rich.
It is time for me
to give up
being a nomad
and develop agriculture.

At five to the third power
I invent
the steam-engine;
at five to the fourth
radio. We need
voices that will thread
between continents.
There are many of us now.
Three thousand, one hundred
and twenty-five of us,
to be exact.
We no longer count
by seasons,
by our fingers.
We have become exact.

At five to the fifth
power, there is
a noise of crying.
Children starve

in the street-gutters.
Power is everywhere.
People who understand it
are drawn past
in rickshaws, holding
the gold abacus
that has become their sign.

The Fisherman's Wife
sitting like a rabbit
in her poor hutch
at the seashore
asked first
for nothing much:
five to the second power.
She bought a
crude eyebrow-pencil.
The magic fish
who allowed this
laughed and laughed.

Later, it was
cloth-of-gold
of tissue, diadems.
It was water-slaves
for the deceived
intricate gardens.
She began to think
in millions.
Those terms.

The world responds to us.
Number by number
undoes itself.
The sea drains.
On the last mud,
still laughing,
lies the magic fish.

## This Mouth Is

This mouth is busiest.
Forgetting to kiss you,
chewing its way through
forty cigarettes,
eating its neighborhood:
one giant chocolate bar,
six figs.

It could be loveable
if it could quit
small-talking bystanders,
chattering away
as if God gave it
the responsibility
for all His silences.

It isn't all of me.
I'm more than it.
I can cross my eyes
when I want to.
When I was only six
I was taught
to tap-dance.

Shut it up.
You know, put
wax in your ears,
the ashtrays
out of reach.
Starve the busybody
into submission.

Make it say O
it has forgotten
what to say.
Then, when it is slack
with surprise,
make love to me
in the sudden quiet.

## At Bablockhythe

The ferry over the Thames had sunk, but a schoolmaster
from Henley, red-eyed, a wild rose in his buttonhole,
took us across in his boat. He insisted that you row,
that you were an American Indian, gently insisted
(as he talked past us into some place we could not see)
that we stop for a drink with him, that we only listen.

We took the narrow path, pitted by cattle hooves,
away from the river, while it began to rain,
and found, almost in the path, a wild rabbit
hunched quietly. He should have run, he should have been afraid,
but his eye was gone. In the shock of that red furrow
he ignored us, moving inward toward his dying.

I wake later and later, red-eyed, slack
in these leaden long-dark mornings, try to pretend
that desires and purposes will use up the day,
but I lose things easily, almost as if I had lost
the idea of what connected me and them,
now you have gone, over sea, into your own journey.

## Therefore

Nothing exists that is not marred; therefore
we are obliged to imagine how things might be:
the sea
at its green uttermost, the shore
white to exaggeration, white before
it was checked and clouded by its spent debris.

Nothing exists that does not end, and so
to knowledge we must deliberately be untrue:
you
murmuring that you will not go, when you will go,
promising to do always what you cannot do:
hold the sun steady, and the sky new.

No one exists who can be loved the same
by day as by dark; it is that sleeping place,
lame,
we attempt to follow into, and cannot trace,
that makes us lie, saying we know his face
as if we knew even half of his true name.

## The Death of Mr. Thrale

When Queeny, his imperious daughter,
found Mr. Thrale stretched out after his stroke, lying
flat on the floor of his house in Grosvenor Square,
she naturally enquired.

"I chuse it," replied Mr. Thrale.
Firmly.
"I lie so a-purpose."

Henry Thrale ate voraciously.
He could abstain from wine, but when he drank
he became without reservation a person drinking.

The little vessels of his head
given their instructions, behaved appropriately.

He died that night. His wife had tried to warn him.
His physicians had tried, Dr. Johnson had tried to warn him.

But finding the smallest grain of the self himself,
entering it, as a man might enter his own seed,
Mr. Thrale had decided.

            Plain, compressed
to a carpet upon the carpet, a human floor,

"I chuse it.
I lie so a-purpose,"
said Mr. Thrale.

# Virginia Woolf Gathers Mushrooms

She is not easy to see. She wears
something anonymous: not the dress
she has not got and so (sigh of relief)
cannot go to the party she was
so much of two minds about going to.
Certainly not the dress she wore down
to dinner at Hyde Park Gate, after
washing in the inadequate basin, the dress
her half-brother, that authority,
looked at and looked away.

The mushrooms are not
really an obsession, but, as the war
keeps killing and removing, as the moon
becomes a mere indicator (if it is bright
there will be German planes, the servants
on mattresses in the basement) there is
little enough to hope for, little
that seems convincing
in any natural way.

Chocolate is unobtainable, eggs arrive
by two, if they arrive. But on the slope
above Asheham, at the right time of the year,
the mushrooms are given. There are the right places
to find them, learned only by craft and care.
Some visitors (Pernel Strachey, Vice-President
of Newnham College, Cambridge) look too high.
The trick is to focus in.

The years gone, it is easy to imagine her,
that historic profile, attending to the best music,
dividing and discriminating, allowed for once
the right dress, the right hat, the clothes
one discriminates in.

Harder

to watch her carry her almost-nothing body
up the earth slope, taking on an earthen color,
vanishing almost from the over-freighted air,
to watch where yesterday
there was nothing; today, something.
In a little dip of the hill, enough mushrooms
to fill her handkerchief, enough
for two people to eat, quietly, at evening,
love continuing, life happening,
the house easy so.

## In the Dreaming

*Indeed, there seems to have been a continual preoccupation
with the mystery of life and death, and all that was unknown
or not present was referred to as being "in the dreaming."*
Alan Moorehead, *The Fatal Impact*

1.

In the dreaming
we walk through the streets of Oxford
hand in hand.
I am able to let you touch me,
to be glad.

Voices laugh around us
in the dark almost dawn
hurrying toward the river
and the May morning.

Perhaps even the ghost
of our unborn child,
male, stirs,
smiles in his twelve-year sleep.

2.

Here, in the summer city
I lie in bed, closing
darkness about my mind,

closing doors, windows,
hiding
where hiding's possible,

not able to taste
in the sky
the weather turning.

3.

At Magagnosc
in the stone bedroom
waked
by some dream of loss

the terraces of vines
steep outside
in the green dark

you came naked to me
through midnight,
frightened and confident,

safe in our same bed.


4.

We meet, eating, smoking,
talking of therapists or friends,
looking through thick glass windows
at the impractical sea.

The seeds of death always between us
on the plastic table.

I try to will myself
not to pick them up.

What do I remember?
You asked once
to be buried beside your mother.


5.

If forgiveness comes
it will be gradual.

Subtle
and loose as smoke.

A little lessening
of this grim year.


6.

Thinking of me,

think of what was

and of what in it
there might have been.

Nothing is thrown away.

Nothing is lost, not
the most awkward kiss,
not
viciousness, rage.

All are still there,
loving you as they can,
wise, in the heart's night,

all there, in the dreaming.

## The Poet's Farewell to His Teeth

Now you are going, what can I do but wish you
(as my wife used to say) "every success
in your chosen field."

What we have seen together! Doctor X,
having gagged us, hurling his forceps to the floor
and denouncing our adolescent politics,

or the time we had caught trench-mouth in Iowa City
and had to drive west slowly and haltingly,
spitting in all the branches of the Missouri.

Cigar-stained and tired of cavities, you leave.
It is time to go back to the pure world of teeth
and rest, and compose yourselves for the last eruption.

As to those things in a glass by the bathroom sink
they will never communicate with me as you have done,
fragile and paranoid, sensing the world around you

as wild drills and destructive caramel, getting even
for neglect by waking me into the pain of dawn,
that empty and intimate world of our bitter sharing.

Go, under that cool light. I will remember you:
the paper reports that people may still feel pain
in their missing teeth, as with any amputation.

I hope you relax by the shadowy root canals,
and thinking of me with kindness, but not regret,
toast me just once in the local anaesthetic.

# Chickens in San Francisco

*San Francisco. You can have four animals total. If you have a*
*dog and a cat, you could only have two chickens.*
*Sunset*, March 1974

In aerobatics, white, red, speckled & spectacular
as if any spot on earth were the pin's bottom
of an enormous cage opening up to chicken heaven,
in a blur of parts, the eyes fringed and knowing,
the oviducts popping white eggs, brown, an eternal Easter,
hens running flat-footed, hysterical, the roosters up
in a little air, down, the scream, contentment,
chickens frying omelets, stuffing feather pillows, whirling
into feather fights, a believable feather winter . . .

| 17

If I kept chickens, that is how I would keep chickens.

Deduct the cat and the dog, which are imaginary,
and you have two chickens, a male chicken and a female chicken
(chicken sexing is high paid work, but you have to travel).
They are walking around the deck. They are Plymouth Rocks.
The male chicken wears a buckled hat and carries a shotgun
and the female chicken has the New England *ABC*:
A is for Abstinence, B is for Boils, C is for Colonel Sanders.
The chickens look terribly sparse on the windy deck,
as if born plucked. They look at each other,
conscious of a hidden camera. They approach a cabbage
and under it they discover Shirley Temple.
They register the salvation of the race.
Shirley clucks a little, she is well into
what they call the skin of the part . . .

Oh cut, cut, cut, cut, cut. I feel about chickens
the opposite of the way San Francisco feels.
I feel about chickens, I feel about other animals
the way Colette felt about truffles. It is no good having any
unless you can have too much.

## The Fool in the Tarot

A dog and a precipice, that's good. The precipice
asks to be fallen down. The dog says no,
keep comfortable, stay in the old ways, I will protect you.

Morning is meant for excitement, a wind like this
lifting the light hair on my arms. I could almost sweat.
The dog is not sure if I even smell the same.

I could let my arms lift, and the cloak, ballooning
out in the free sky would take me from my fixed feet.
The permission is on me like sex, melting and melting.

How intact dogs are. Refusing to be human
they will keep a blind boy from falling over a cliff
even when his best dream makes him in love with falling.

How do you explain that zero is not a number?
I am the unbroken egg of all the numbers.
I cannot divide even in my dividing mind.

The wind exciting my fingers, I pet my dog.
We are all as young as each other, or as the day.
I am still, containing selves. I am being happy.

# Die Alte Frau, Die Alte Marschallin

Of the three voices, it is hers that stays.

The lovers leave the stage. They have become
a shape of their own, perhaps not a lasting one
but enough for now.

Who does not know their world,
the thrones, the feasts,
the wealth and accomplishment that warm like day?
Who has not slept in that bed, made out of the breasts
of nightingales? Who has not touched
delicacy so ideal it is feather, neither bone?

But they have left. The stage now is hers alone.

She has been them, to come here. She has sung
innocent Sophie, Octavian the youthful lover.
Girl to young man to someone who is outside sex.
*Die alte Frau, die alte Marschallin.*
The old woman, the old woman who is in love.

But then with what, we ask, because she is alone
on the stage. Is it that she loves herself?
Is it, God forbid, her impertinent Negro page?
Is it age? We might understand that affair,
love gestures stroking unresponsive air,
smiles that make smiling into an offense,
that loss of sense to sense.

No, dear, it is the music, the generosity.
She is in the music alone, it is her place.
She has come to it out of her romances:
girl, boy, the carrier of the silver rose,
the prince of chances.
Now she folds into herself. It is her repose.
She advances.

Having had the stage to herself, she lets it go.
For a moment everything is empty. Her page,
quick as an eyelash, comes on to recover
her handkerchief.

                    Somewhere, a lover
turns in the night, knowing that he will age.

We know, we know, love. Here is the empty stage.

Two
The Rainbow Grocery

## What I Want

I want to be mentioned more. I want to be able
to be dramatic: a sculptured Renaissance mouth
fifteen feet high. I want all the pistol fingers.
I want to drive up in a Bentley as big as a boat.

I'd like somebody to see to this pretty quickly.

## Appearance in Public Places

Entertain us, said the chairman
of the board of supervisors
and I went into this low dance.
I was never more embarrassed.

I am supposed to have learned
propriety at my mother's knee
but it was so absolute I could never
see into the clouds at its summit.

This is my tambourine, and these are my white
fangs I made myself out of collar-stays.
I laugh and laugh. I hope it covers up
the municipal judges.

Oh! the undignified rouge!
Thank God that, over the whole expanse
of tongues waiting behind articulated teeth
night seems to be falling.

Killing to Eat

*The serious cook really must face up to the task personally.*
*. . . Using a sharp knife or lobster shears, cut straight down ½*
*inch into the back of the lobster, at the point where tail and*
*chest join, thus severing the spinal cord and killing the lobster*
*instantly.*
Julia Child and Simone Beck, *Mastering the Art of French*
*Cooking, II*

In the kitchen sink, two dozen astonished crayfish
crawl over each other to claw at the stainless steel.
I am a serious cook, and I will kill them.
Preparing a bath of vinegar, vegetables, spices,
I bring it to a boil and plunge them in.
They die instantly. They oblige me
by turning, in three minutes, pure Chinese red.

Later that night I wake, half out of dream,
and reach for the bedside glass that has my Sign,
the Archer, on it. Bewildered, I seem to see
not the Sign but one of the crayfish, resurrected,
climbing the inside of my glass to get in touch.

In the backyard of the house on Nelson Street
there was a chopping block and a Boy Scout hatchet
for killing the Sunday chickens. The hen picked up
out of her flock, the accurate glittering blow.
I watched one of them cut up. Inside, for tomorrow,
a completed egg, then one that was not quite finished,
then a dozen others, smaller to microscopic,
crowding her oviduct.

In our Zodiac there is no Sign
of Hen, or Cow, or Pig. It is full of hunters.
Orion stalks our sky with his Dogs, his Bears.
Underneath them scrabbles the eater, Cancer.

25

Could there be a kitchen Zodiac, in which
the Sign of the virgin Egg, the reclusive Lobster,
climb up the sky? Where we locate north
by looking for the constellation of the Bruised Calf?
Where, after we have uneasily crossed the equator,
the constellation of the Southern Fish is rising?

We wake from that dream sweating, nothing resolved.
The galaxy is the shape of an eating mouth.
The Wolf salivates in the vacuum, the Snake engorges.
We must eat to live, and we must kill to eat.

The serious cook will always face this problem.

## Androids

Androids
are not different in appearance
from you and me
except they are more beautiful.
Male-type androids are muscular,
have smooth chests
and incredible apparatus;
the female-type
are, as we say, pneumatic,
and have been taught everything about it
there is to know.

You have been to bed
with an android, probably thinking
"Jesus, did I luck out!" The android
is not really thinking about you at all.
It is gathering information
for the data bank.

As you fall back,
exhausted, unsuspicious,
the android will kiss your forehead.
It will murmur "Thank you."
And then it will leave.
It is a characteristic of androids
not to stay on till morning.

And even if you *were* suspicious
it would do you little good.
The only way to identify the android
is to look inside its navel
where it is stamped
with its country of manufacture.

That is why it leaves while you are exhausted.
It is important to it
not to let you get that close.

# The Raft of the *Medusa*

*To the memory of William Chaplin*

1.

I kissed you, at a party. I was drunk.
You were tall and blond and young, and very much surprised.
You must have thought no one would want to kiss you.

What was it, beautiful, that you held
so entirely to yourself? The gun in your body
waiting for all those years to charge itself?
Your music that would not let itself be music?

And so at the various parties, aloof,
surprised, of course surprised you were even living.
The circumflex of your eyebrow, the long smile . . .
It has taken me these five years to write about you.
How wrong! my libretto can only say, How wrong!

2.

We are for weeks floating in the Atlantic
on the raft of the *Medusa*, everyone
who has been saved from the wreck crouching
on that piece of board.
The sea is unkindly neutral: no gulls, no island.
Yet we are somehow in the office, the supervisor
in her lacquered hair, the time-clock simpering,
everything clashing and clashing against the hour.

And the hour will strike. We, passengers,
look hungrily at each other as the voyage continues.
When there is no food at all, we will eat each other.
I you; you me. Let me push you off this raft
into the at least natural violence of the ocean.
Let me drag you out of the ocean, let me do
something for you, what you never let me do.

In Gericault's mind, it is a composition.
He can allow it because it balances.
He can shrug, say: "That is the way it was."
It seems to be, truly, the way it is.
There is no way
I can reach back to touch you, mind or body.
I have read the poems you left, and they are bad.


3.

Night in the museum. Your picture gathers
a little light, but it sinks mostly into
its baroque frame, the dark varnish, things that allow
me to suppose you were never in my life.
But you were! You must have been! I kissed you!

Tall, blond, as the remote light gathers
everyone who is lost, as the mind tries to gather
everyone who has died, as Gericault's hurt raft
gathers to itself on that indifferent ocean,
I cannot wholly believe that is the way it is.

I am persuaded, and I am not persuaded.
There was every need and no need for you to die.

## The Food of Love

I could never sing. In the grade-school operetta
I sat dark offstage and clattered coconut shells.
I was the cavalry coming, unmusical, lonely.

For five years I played the piano and metronome.
I read *Deerslayer* in small print while I waited for my lesson,
and threw up after the recital at the Leopold Hotel.

I went to a liberal college, but I never learned
how to sit on the floor or help the sweet folk song forward.
My partridge had lice, and its pear-tree had cut-worm blight.

Yet this song is for you. In your childhood a clear falsetto,
now you sing along in the bars, naming old songs for me.
Even drunk, you chirrup; birds branch in your every voice.

It's for you, what I never sing. So I hope if ever
you reach, in the night, for a music that is not there
because you need food, or philosophy, or bail,

you'll remember to hear the noise that a man might make
if he were an amateur, clattering coconut shells,
if he were the cavalry, tone-deaf but on its way.

## Letter from Hawaii

I wish I could huddle like sleep into your body,
be where you smell, watch you carry your ass naked
through the whole high house. I wish I could kiss you:
firmness, slow giving way, open. I wish I could suck your tongue.

Where you are not, there's death; the Nembutal
plays with itself on the cheap coffee table.
The Japanese tourists and the tropical sea
torment each other. Why should I interrupt them?

You're the only one in my life I've beaten up
and you lay there not hitting back, not understanding.
Was that love? Is that love? The brute pacific distance
overwhelming you when you know I want to kill?

There will be noise all night: rock radio
and the loose door banging and banging. Valentine,
listen with what has happened to your body.
Let me hear from you, so that the morning comes.

## It Will Come Right

Day after day
you move my furniture
where you think
you want it.
You bring home
indecipherable things
from garage sales
and exhibit them

and No! I cry, No!
You have to be *like* me.
I can tolerate
only my mirror brother,
my identical.

You luxuriate in yourself.
Night comes.
You let yourself snore.
That too offends me.

But hour beyond hour
I am patient.
I package your edges.
Each time you are
smaller, less like
what you said you were.
Each time you look
at me uneasily
the moon flickers,
and I invent
more of you
in the space between.

It will come right.
Waxy flexibility,
your hands left
in the attitude

where I left them,
your nakedness
like a smooth doll
waiting for the attachment
of its personal parts.

Finally it will be
love, when I settle
into you
as into an armchair
that is almost human,
when I remember,
indulgently,
as from a distance,
even the things you were
before you gave yourself
to the new start.

## Sheena the Outcast Drag Queen

In a shore apartment
on Waikiki,
a hundred yards from the surf,
Sheena the Outcast Drag Queen
does her number,
emerges dancing from
the door of her bedroom closet.

It is the only entrance
and the only audience
she can still extort.

And God how bad she is!
How poor, meagre!
Grey color of old
gunmetal on the thin body;
scratched,
sprinkled with hairs.

As if the door to a womb opened
and something with a cane
and a straw hat
and no mouth to speak of
came out, realizing
how it would fail.

That vast bed,
the Pacific night,
swings at the window,
makes itself into sexes.
Even the tourists' limbs
lock into sex, sleep.
Fish leap
into phosphorescence.

Narrow as a nail, voice
like a dog in a phonograph,

but a mean dog,
Sheena the Outcast
Drag Queen, in her closet
of a coffin breathes,
screams,
emerges,
beats up the vulnerable.
Ages.

The sound of the music
forces her
and from the narrow door
that is her place to live
she tries to live.

She opposes the whole sea,
the moon,
the music.

She is the only thing she knows.

She is her art.

# Alligators and Paris and North America

*For Adrianne on her birthday*

Bernice Dewey *going to the Snyder trial, then coming back
and hypnotizing her alligator, which she kept in the tub and
which Dos Passos said was rather limp from having been hyp-
notized so much.*

No, darling, the world is not ruled by sense, not sense.
For every statue of George Washington making laws
in every city, there is in some back room
Bernice Dewey hypnotizing her alligator,
she intent and glittering, the uneasy reptile
hoping it is all a dream, that it will wake
back in the Everglades.

                    I walked down Stockton
Street toward Market. It was a reasonable day.
But when I looked to my right, there walking beside me
was a six-foot carrot, quite casual, taking the air.
I looked helplessly to my left, to a six-foot mushroom.
It was no time for composure. I almost ran.
Nobody had told me about the new health-food store
that was opening that day. Turning onto Stockton,
coming up to meet me in the most deliberate way
were two men sitting inside a large football helmet.
I caught a bus and went home. It was not my day.

Darling, not sense. I don't know why it is.
But why, when the plastic zipper of my trousers broke
in the I. Magnin dressing room, and the disdainful attendant
gave me four brass safety-pins to put myself back together,
and you asked him what was taking so long, why did he say
"I'm afraid, Madam, that he has had an accident." *That* day
I went back to the parking garage and backed the car
straight into a pillar. An attendant on a Moped
looked at me curiously and drove away.

*Having acquired the necessary training, Mary Cassatt was hung*
*in the prestigious Paris Salon for five consecutive years, no mean*
*distinction for any painter, let alone an American woman.*

I know he is right. If he had meant hanged
he would have *said* hanged, yet I cannot help seeing her
with resistless decorum through those five long years,
her skirts neat and even her feet held
effortlessly in the first position of ballet,
hanging on the museum wall. What would be
"the necessary training" and how would one acquire it?
Perhaps in a Paris studio, day by day
inching a little farther up the wall,
doing Yoga to help it all, pulling away
mentally and physically from the unnecessary floor.
If our lives are supposed to be art, that would be one way:
to become the picture. It would be "no mean distinction."
You are an American woman. What would you say?

*My earliest episode of conscious frigidity—that is, of frigidity*
*after the fact of accepting my homosexuality and after spells*
*of being comfortable with it—occurred in a bathtub on 17th*
*and Market Streets in San Francisco . . .*

There it is, the bathtub motif recurs.
The limp alligator, the limp homosexual. Are we all hypnotized?
What is that bathtub doing in the street—
a busy intersection, as it happens,
where all of the streetcars turn?

Conscious frigidity. It sounds like something
achieved, rather than come across by chance.
This is my friend, Conscious Frigidity.
He/she is an avatar of Shiva the Destroyer.
I am happy to meet you, Avatar. I hope you can drink vodka.
There is an alligator in the bathroom named Bernice Dewey.
I mean the *bathroom* is named Bernice Dewey.
For some reason the alligator keeps trying to escape.
Even to hypnotism, it keeps saying, there must be an end.

Friend, if you are friend, take me away.
Let us sail this bathtub straight out of 17th and Market
into the awakening day.

*When he went on to sing* I send thee a gift of roses, *however,
and attempted to cast some artificial flowers into the audi-
ence, the wire stems got caught in his bodice, so that he had
to keep pulling at them—like something in a dream, Bodfish
said, when all your powers become paralyzed and you can't
accomplish anything.*

Roses were the wrong choice. No wonder the wires got caught
like something in a dream.

                              I dreamed of reason
in the way that Goya did, and found the same
ruin, the same pitilessness, the same shame.
It is not sense, darling, that regulates us.
If I offer you flowers, are they flowers that can speak their name?
Or does it matter, as long as they are not tame?

Now it is spring, the camellias are in bloom.
On the sheltered deck, the Japanese maple
puts out new leaves as if it had perfect faith.
How does a flower feel when it tries to break
from its still internal shape?
How does a leaf feel its shape, as the closed fan stretches?
Like a man stretching his arms up into the air,
yawning, yawning so loud it is pure vigor,
brings the hair to attention, prick
to alertness, eyes sidling around the bar the old way.
Darling, not sense, but something that has its say.

The wire stems caught in his bodice. I could cry.
He is trying so, and so failing as he tries.
I see him with his eyes
averted, and with a sick flush rising.
He has done it *wrong*. There was the advertizing
and now he has messed it up. It was not his day.
It is nonsense. It was nonsense from the start.
Defeated, determined, dead.

And still, for all of its awkwardness, sincere.
A fool being a fool in his own way.

> Margaret's uncle had invested in $10,000 worth of fireworks
> and set them off in the Bois de Boulogne, and then killed him-
> self. (Dorothy Parker said, when I told her about this: "And
> those bum French fireworks—probably only a fourth of them
> went off!") An aunt used to sit at her window and drop ink on
> people in the street.

It is not sense. Why do I keep expecting that?
The mad old aunt
drops ink (Ink?) on the people in the street.
Where does she get the ink? A trust fund, maybe.
It is the same wild kind of determination.
Bernice Dewey hypnotizing her alligator, the old aunt
deliberately, close in on target, dropping ink.
I imagine she would have chosen dove-grey hats,
or the shoulders of very expensive prostitutes
who would look at their carefully-powdered shoulders, think
"I have done wrong." Or that is what she would think.
Sleeps well at night, like anyone with a plan.

Tonight, ten thousand dollars worth
of fireworks will destroy the Bois de Boulogne.
Clutching the last rocket, there will be a mad old man
trying to get to Heaven if he can.
He will have spent
the whole damn heritage, down to the last *pour-boire*.
All to have fire. It is not sense at all.
But the fire-fall
climbs to its ultimate, destroys, descends.
It has its own bright ends.
So near, so far.
All that we are, and what we think we are.

(Quotations in the poems are from: Edmund Wilson, *The Twenties*,
ed. Leon Edel; John Barkham, a review in the *San Francisco
Chronicle*; G. J. Hoisington, an article in *Gay Sunshine*.)

# The Shortest Day

*To the memory of Ralph Dickey*

The white room that I eat in and write in
is filled with the wet light of a winter afternoon.
It is the shortest day.

Tangerines, lemons,
bright yellow candles in bright lacquer holders.
I use these to hold on with. To try.

You yourself have taken your darkness away with you
and somewhere in this wet enormous country now
you are lying, as thin as you could ever have wished to be.

It is a little harder, here, without you.
The light lessens, and the voices of shouting children
distance themselves in the ending of this cold year.

Be at some ease. We will come walking toward you,
seeking you, to kneel clumsily, to lie down,
to move a little, until the wet earth lets us in.

Now, for you, I am lighting a candle, and another,
so as to kill myself not this night, but another.
But that is only time. When it needs to, the joining will come.

I wish I could ask you to wait for me
there where you are in the night, at least touch my hand,
at least say to me, "Quiet, now. Come in."

# The Rainbow Grocery

You don't find it for yourself. Someone takes you.
The bars have shut down and still it is not time.
Whatever was going to happen is lost in the smoke
and the old booze, of the people who made it leaving together.
Of the quiet that comes when you've said it. Nothing to say.
That's the time of night for The Rainbow Grocery.

And it looks like nothing, like nowhere on God's earth,
like an old place abandoned. It is abandoned,
but the abandoned door opens, onto a lobby
of wax derelicts, grey as the uncertain night.
No one human has sat in these chairs. No one human.
The lights are yellow and they are ready to die.

You pay a dollar to get in. Then
there's a place to check your valuables. Then
there is a dusty hall which might lead: where?
Then down a staircase to a grimy basement.
You can get coffee or soft drinks if you really want them.
That's the room where men are dancing only with men.

Past that is what it's all about: the black room.
You walk past its door and you know it's full of people,
people you can't see and were never meant to see,
hands touching you, chests, bellies, the shy night.
And if you are stripped, sucked, and the rest done to you,
The Rainbow Grocery will have taken you in.

Always at the end of a hall, of a dark hall
where there is a next room, always, a next room,
and who knows what's sleeping there, then or forever?
Always when the bars close, somebody says:
"Why don't we go down to The Rainbow Grocery?
You haven't been there? I can get you in."

Three
Face-Paintings

## Happiness

I sent you this bluebird of the name of Joe
with "Happiness" tattooed onto his left bicep.
(For a bluebird, he was a damn good size.)
And all you can say is you think your cat has got him?

I tell you the messages aren't getting through.
The Golden Gate Bridge is up past its ass in traffic;
tankers colliding, singing telegrams out on strike.
The machineries of the world are raised in anger.

So I am sending this snail of the name of Fred
in a small tricolor sash, so the cat will know him.
He will scrawl out "Happiness" in his own slow way.
I won't ever stop until the word gets to you.

## The Revival of Vaudeville

I don't think this is going to work,
Maud said, jamming herself into the cannon.
I've gained weight.

I tried to spell anthropomorphic
all over the range
of my teeth.

Love, your magic spell is everywhere.

He *was* circumcised, but before he was converted,
so I think they had to bring this Rabbi in
and do it all over again. It was only a tiny snip, though.
It shows what you have to go through to be Orthodox.

If it won't fit, Maud said, screw it.
I did but
she was never the same girl afterwards.

Love, your tragic smell is everywhere.

Can you pick out 16 things in this picture that do not fit?
There is a horse with 16 legs wearing lace garters.

Denis, I think you must be insane, she cried,
whipping the shreds of lace from her foaming bosom.

What do you mean, the cannon goes with me? Maud said.
You think a girl can make out in a singles bar these days
wearing a cannon?

Giancarlo, Giancarlo, why have you left me?
High tides are flooding the pigeons in the Piazza San Marco.
It is lost, that little tune on the harpsichord.

Love, your pelagic swell is everywhere.

Listen, Maud, I said, just tell them
you were fired with enthusiasm.

Now, while the 16 horses are dancing the schottische,
it it time we threw the babies out of the troika,
it is time we escaped across the Lithuanian frontier.

## Show Biz

Listen, lately I have not been entertained
by this lousy TV party called This Is Your Life
given me by an old glacier whose tits droop.

It was supposed to be old friends, old friends:
the vodka bottle from the bottom right-hand drawer,
the condoms in primary colors, including black.

I was ready to laugh and cry as the show demanded,
embrace the inflatable sponsor, lick, drool,
be naked except for my well-known diamond crotch.

All, all misunderstood. These dull faces
saying "I love you. I wish you would let me love you."
That, Desdemona, is not what I mean by show biz.

And as soon as I can get out of this studio
I am going to have my body hair plucked to spell
"Fuck You" and I am having the whites of my eyes dyed younger.

And that will take care of those faces, the blunt sadness,
the destruction of being human, the things I never
never in this world would have signed the contract for.

## George

Name it, name it, name it.
Name it George.
Name it after a disaster.
George was a disaster.
Is that close enough?
Name it Clever.
Clever was a disaster.

Holding my great fat
fingers out in the dawn sun
I walk about
stepping on the flowers,
spitting.
Where I spit
there is a flower with a name.

Name me, name me, name me.
Your name is Ed.
You are going to grow up
to be a dictionary.
Your name is Alice
and you will grow up queer.
Your name is
Nothing-at-All
and what will become of you
not even your mother
Everything-at-All
knows for sure.

See?
It is what happens to you,
little one, soft one,
it is what happens to you
after you start
learning about names.

## The Visit to Fresno

It was after the visit to Fresno that he became aloof.
His researches in the erenteenth century had always occupied
a good deal of his time, and his students, and the pottery
gnomes he kept making and making for his friends' gardens.
It was as if he had opened his hands and let them drop.

He seems not to have spoken all through Easter week
and not to have written, though he gave fingerprints
to those who asked for them, as long as he had any.
He spent much of his time near the radio, building
what appeared to be a trap for the emerging words.

No one was actually there when he took root
in the window box. We were sorry, but we had been delayed.
I had had a real problem with the thermometers,
Oral and Rectal. He was oblivious to our efforts,
except that he spelled out "Geranium" in Braille.

As it goes, so it has been. Harold asks
that I say a word of thanks to the many contributors,
including the indefatigable Mr. McMath, without whose.
And of course the London Library, and the typists.
But my greatest debt is owing to X, my wife.

We are agreed that his condition has stabilized
and that that frees us to be indiscreet
which we shall be when we have got it organized.
Meanwhile we do not have much real evidence to go on
unless by "Geranium" he said more than he meant to say.

# Someone is Looking for Jack

I would like things to be nice but they aren't going to.
Every day I will get two phone calls from my ex-lover
accusing me of meanness and frigidity,
and every day one phone call asking for Jack
from a black who doesn't believe this is not Jack's number.

I could have an unlisted phone put in and probably
get all of the calls from everyone's ex-lover
accusing me under many names of frigidity
and meanness, and there would be a whole generation
of lost angry voices always trying to reach Jack.

Sometimes I begin to wonder if I am Jack
or was Jack in some unspeakable episode
and wandered around the city writing my number
on the walls of restrooms, with obscene suggestions.
I hope not. I never wanted to be pathetic.

I keep thinking the right calls must be *in* the phone
if I knew how to find them: an invitation to lunch
at the Relais de la Campagne, State Farm Insurance
saying that all my debts have caught fire and burned,
or a voice translating a poem into Greek.

I keep thinking I will lift the phone and get in touch
with that other world behind this world, where voices
are the voices of stone and grass, where telephones
grow naturally at the natural banks of rivers,
where hello is a place with birds in it, and sings.

But so far all I get is heavy breathing,
or a recorded message on frigidity
and meanness, or from too near a black voice saying:
"You call the company, man, you got some trouble.
I called your number last week and I talked to Jack."

# Telemachus

## 1.

You are grown up, surely it is time for you
to set off and look for your father, who is missing.
You have had photographs, but they were taken
by the family, mostly in black-and-white.
Those who knew him, women especially,
say: "He was better looking.
You would have had to see him yourself."
They flutter their fans.
Resentfully, they say:
"There is nothing here that does him justice."

You are over six foot yourself, and well set-up.
Nothing has been lacking in your education.
But it is not for you they languish and decline
in their silken reveries, it is not for you
that their eyes soften, mouths tickle with remembrance.
They think of someone they are jealous of in time.

Up to now, you have hardly been in time.
For twenty years, the sea has been a bowl,
still, permanent, in which the island sat.
The ladies were so many courtesy aunts,
the suitors people who for her own amusement
your mother entertains. They can be woven
into her habitual account of day upon day:
those webs in which you are peripheral, or missing.

Without announcement, you will find yourself
in a small boat, launched into an actual Ocean.
If you look for hands, there will be only two.
If you think, you are the mirror of your thinking.
Your skin burns, your hair bleaches from the salt.
Any sail you put up has your own name marked upon it.
In the wake you leave, the waves rehearse
and forget you.

The Ocean is empty, but there are always
landfalls. Arriving at evening, no water left,
sailing by a difficult strait into the harbor,
you will find, always, your father has been there before you.
In one village they will tell you that they ate him,
but they are not convincing, their eyes shift.
In another port
you will find his image in a mud phallic god.
Always the ladies,
holding up the bronze mirror, rouging their nipples,
will say of him: "How could I not remember?"
Out of remembering, they will take you to their beds
where he has been before you.
It is hard to imagine a place he has not been.

2.

You must sail into another Ocean, outside
the possible world: a frozen
incumbrance of a place, ice monuments
breaking and re-forming, the song of the tall ice.
If there are inhabitants, they do not speak
any of the supple tongues you have picked up, voyaging.
They neither remember you nor remember him.
They sing into your mind: "He is not here."
Images flicker and dance in the inhuman sky:
it might be your father, but it is only image.
You have arrived beyond the end of the world.
You have yourself, otherwise there is nothing here.

Even into these waters, Summer comes.
A short slackening of the ice
out of which your boat goes free, unguided.
You are interior to the wave, you are yourself.
Being is not a comfort, but an instruction.
As you move north, you civilize
the islands: these are people who could be men.
They incline to you, recognizing the change
in your face. They offer their daughters to you,
none of whom has lain with a man. They cry: "Change!"
What they see, looking at you, effects it.

Months, perhaps years later, after meeting
with easy indifference women with the feet of birds,
women with dogs barking from their bellies, you return
to the place you set out from, a place
difficult to remember.

Old women come down to the beach. Their fans have rotted.
Suitors come down, but they have now no swords.
Your mother comes. She does not know what to say
after all this time. Her eyes have blurred
with the years, even in that place of long-woven calm.
She finds you hard to recognize. "Welcome, Son?"
she says with uncertainty. "Welcome, Husband?"

## His Death from Cancer

I dig my foot into the stubborn grass.
I look to where the stellar jays, by two,
figure in anger about their threatened nest.
He, a high shape of water, walks
across his attentive lawn and disappears.

Let us make, in fear, a disarray
of the sheets, let us make love until
it is hard to tell which breath comes from which body.
Nipple to nipple, let us exhaust the clock
until no time is available for his going.

I will make him, as with no preliminaries
I explore you, live. I will make him
a language it is not possible not to talk in.
I will bring him to the bewilderment of being.
I will be fed by him, I will be fed.

The grass abstains. It knows when it is evening.
And you lie back, your muscles lessening towards
anatomy. All the birds of the beleaguered air
hum into their light-belled bones and hang asleep.
It is the accountant's hour.

The construction of memory begins. Now there, now here,
I half-realize his absence, as we lie
counting the generations, recognizing
how alone it is to be the oldest living,
unprotected against the hard newness of the sky.

# After Two Years of Analysis: Reactions

I went twice a week to the Black Minds Monument
where sculptors in the largest scale had blasted her
out of the living rock. She had a head
you would not believe. It was hieroglyphic.
And when it spoke, though it never spoke, I imagined
the voice came up from the anus under Delphi
and said, I am the mother you have profaned.
I was all echo. As soon as I was, it rained.

To cry is to begin to become human.
It initiates a flow: eye, sinus, bowel,
the tongue like a flush flooding from the mouth's sphincter.
The man in Agamemnon melts to a bath,
is indistinguishable from the bath, the blooded water.
The woman that was has become an erect stone.

Who has whose body in this double head?
After a time, it becomes harder to tell
technique from history. Is this the counter-transference
or the counter-Reformation? Red female popes,
snakes at their naked breasts, red throbbing mitres.
As we become unbelievable, we merge
to the grave attention of a professional child.

At the bottom of hell, the tourist buses squeeze
with their cameras between grave frozen identities,
not ambisexual merely, but without fixed shape,
that might be reptiles, the ghosts of ideas of birds.
It is narrow here, at the head's entrance, the birth canal.
The bus barely scrapes through, the brakes not holding.
We take quick pictures of what might be the stars.

And having passed, buy postcards for souvenirs.
Mine shows me naked in a brothel with a mirrored ceiling,
hardly knowing what to do with those girls, if they are girls.
Hers shows the Emperor in a Byzantine mosaic,
hieratic, holding a wisdom in his blue hand.

Freud wrote to H.D. to ask her if it was she
who had sent him the white carnations. Was it carnations?
My memory is failing for this kind of exact detail.
They may have been stone carnations, they may have been
the knave and queen of the suit of stone carnations.
But I know it was, in some way, a reconciliation.
And what that implies: a shutting of the right doors.

Conclude. Operating from extinct languages,
from the slightest move of a finger that may be
sanctifying or obscene, we arrive at hesitation.
Suicide is for this month by law suspended.
We must separate. It is too dangerous to go on.
But the light of common morning defines the foothills
where there are caves of early religious sects,
containing scrolls, that have waited a thousand years,
not for triumph, but only for a small adventure:
for the first letter to be unrolled and read.

## On His Way Home to Wyoming

We were too brief to expect to keep in touch.
The traffic stream has carried you past my stop.
I am no time you should remember much:
the moment of tenderness your mind lets drop
the way a cigarette falls from the hand
of a lover who is drunk or half asleep
and harmlessly burns out. I understand
the pleasure of having what we need not keep.

And when you leave, I understand the pleasure
of silence, of having my body to myself,
of washing your glass and putting it on a shelf,
of measuring out the day to my own measure,
at ease, not glad, not sorry that you have gone,
the bed stripped bare, the clean sheets not yet on.

## A Kindness

Where did we stop? In dead summer, that is
male, yellow. You stripped into that glare
of live gold.
It was like living in gold to try to touch you.
It was as if you were day.

Nothing of this is true, but will you
let me have it, Imaginary?

The laugh, confidence, the symmetrical clean
body capable of itself, so being body
as to be naked even to the hands. Will you give me that?

Because even if it is not true, I need
something now to look back to, in order to say:
I have been sudden in the sun's perfection,
I have had blood rise like light,
my hands have answered,
my memory is a bush of grown flame.

It is a kindness you can do me, to have been there
at the center of summer, yourself the attack of summer,
and to have made all that light out of being young.

I need to have loved you. I need to have told you so.

# The Heroine

*Here we heard that captains of schooners which had arrived
from Hawaii, report that a light is visible on the terminal crater
of Mauna Loa, 14,000 feet above the sea, that Kilauea, the
flank crater, is unusually active, and that several severe shocks
of earthquake have been felt. This is exciting news.*
Isabella L. Bird, *Six Months in the Sandwich Islands*

She arrives at the volcano almost dead,
the enormous modesty of her skirts, torn, drenched, dragging her
    back,
and the sickness, whatever it is she travels to get away from,
    preventing her.
The rocks, the rain, the night relapse into violence,
into the self-centered brutality of an adolescent world.
She has to go there.

Her family is good. She is of independent means.
The missionaries respect her.
And she *does* believe. Those are in fact real psalms
in which she participates, a real God living in loving-kindness,
justice made merciful, with a truly Christian people.
In the midst of that, the mouth of the night demands her

and she must go, with an unsympathetic woman, not English,
and a guide partly reluctant, part threatening,
part not determinable, into the chaotic lava,
flows, tubes, a landscape of black intestines
that has hardened only the moment she looked at it.
She must go beyond that
to where it is all change.

Later on, to the mild surprise of her friends, she will contract
a suitable marriage. Her husband will be
something of an invalid, but not tedious about it.
Inheld by the intricate whalebone of her convention
she will, the heroine, accepting concede herself

into age, into a world it is hard to say
she had abandoned . . .

who still
in that western ocean that went on forever
had not been able not to go to encounter
an entire whale hanging for a miraculous second
in necessary, unsupportive air, before it crashed back
like an explosion into what we think of
as its natural element . . .

who still
in that other necessary part of her mind and place
had moved restlessly, encumbered, across those thousands of miles
to sit in a raw town almost outside the world,
waiting for news from the interior
of what, for her life, she was obliged to see:

the rightness of an extreme, the island burning.

## Honolulu

When I had a beard I could
retire into it.
It was like an ovenbird's nest,
clumsy outwardly,
smooth, intimate
on the inside.
I shaved off the beard
before Honolulu.
It will be too hot, I said.
Bears migrate, I said.
They become people when
they take off their fur
and everybody is overcome
with embarrassment.

It *was* hot
in Honolulu
and I had this face
I didn't know what to do with.
Long reading
had made it into
an eighteenth-century face.
It was only good
for a family portrait
with horses and dogs.

So I have lost weight
and all my friends say
with admiration
"You are unrecognizable.
Until you began talking
we had no idea."

It is not me.
It is a cunningly-made
cast-aluminum android
with reflective surfaces.

It is the King of Hearts
huddled into
plate-armor.
It is the statue
of the Comendador
getting down from its pedestal
to the statue music.

It is Onion Foo-Yung,
devious as opium,
dropping the bodies
through a trap door
into the reeking Thames.
It is a Greek lizard
dropping its tail
so the enemy
has something to play with.

Hurrah!
A band is coming down the street
playing the national anthem,
giving out beards
to infants in highchairs,
thrusting beards
with a high forceps
onto fetuses in the womb.

Everyone says
"You are unrecognizable."
How good that is!
I can leave for Honolulu
to live under a palm tree,
happy,
under an assumed name.

# Face-Paintings of the Caduveo Indians

The face-paintings of the Caduveo, says Levi-Strauss,
reflect a society they have forgotten:
like heraldry, he says, like playing cards.

It is like that. Even my mother, now,
turning the pages of the photograph album,
forgets the older faces. She insists she remembers,
but what she remembers is a style of face,
a way she can remember people looking.

I saw you at the Greek Orthodox church on Sunday.
You had lost weight. I was drinking sweetened coffee.
We were no longer a society.
I saw you as a stranger might, with interest.
You had drawn back behind the surface of your face.

In the last days, having nothing in common, we played cards,
and the cards became their own society,
playing themselves, not responsible to the players.
Your face was new, as if it had not been used.

I do not know what became of the Caduveo.
The face-paintings are in a museum, with the relics
of other societies that forgot themselves,
that became too few to be able to remember.

It is like that: a lessening of chances,
the thought that I will never again be in love
but will sit foolishly waiting for what is in the cards
while your face becomes a photograph, becomes
only a way I remember people looking.

THE
JUNIPER
PRIZE

This volume is the fourth recipient
of the Juniper Prize,
presented annually by the
University of Massachusetts Press
for a volume of original poetry.
The prize is named in honor of Robert Francis,
who has lived for many years at
Fort Juniper, Amherst, Massachusetts.

Library of Congress Cataloging in Publication Data
Dickey, William
The rainbow grocery.
Poems.
I. Title.
PS3507.I28R3  1979  811'.5'4  78-53381
ISBN 0-87023-252-5
ISBN 0-87023-253-3 pbk.